Mommy, Am I Strong?

Written by
Michelle S. Lazurek

Illustrated by
Scott Spinks

Pauline
BOOKS & MEDIA
Boston

Library of Congress Cataloging-in-Publication Data

Lazurek, Michelle S., author.
   Mommy, am I strong? / written by Michelle S. Lazurek ; illustrated by Scott Spinks.
      pages cm
   Audience: Ages 4-7
   ISBN 978-0-8198-4948-9 (pbk.) -- ISBN 0-8198-4948-0 (pbk.)
   1. Boys--Conduct of life--Juvenile literature. 2. Christian life--Juvenile literature. 3.
Conduct of life--Juvenile literature. I. Spinks, Scott, illustrator. II. Title.
   BV4541.3.L39 2015
   248.8'2--dc23
                                        2015011420

This is a work of fiction. Names, characters, places, events, and incidents are either the products of the author's imagination or used in a fictitious manner. Any resemblance to actual persons, living or dead, or actual events is purely coincidental.

The Scripture quotations contained herein are from the *New Revised Standard Version Bible: Catholic Edition*, copyright © 1989, 1993, Division of Christian Education of the National Council of the Churches of Christ in the United States of America. Used by permission. All rights reserved.

Design by Mary Joseph Peterson, FSP

Illustrations by Scott Spinks

"P" and PAULINE are registered trademarks of the Daughters of St. Paul.

Published by Pauline Books & Media, 50 Saint Pauls Avenue, Boston, MA 02130–3491

Printed in the U.S.A.

MAIS VSAUSAPEOILL6-3010047 4948-0

www.pauline.org

Pauline Books & Media is the publishing house of the Daughters of St. Paul, an international congregation of women religious serving the Church with the communications media.

1 2 3 4 5 6 7 8 9   19 18 17 16 15

"I can do all things through Christ
who strengthens me."

See Philippians 4:13

To Caleb,
Be courageous, for when you are weak,
the Lord will make you strong.

Courageous Caleb was a little boy who lived in an ordinary house on an ordinary street.

But there was nothing ordinary about Caleb.

Caleb was a superhero. Or at least he *thought* he was.

He loved to watch his favorite superheroes on TV. Then he would spend hours running around the house, making zooming noises and pretending to fly.

One day Caleb and his cousin, David, were playing at Caleb's house. The two boys took out their superhero capes and put them on. Then they flew into the kitchen and screeched to a stop in front of Caleb's mommy.

"Look how strong I am!" said David, showing her his big muscles.

Caleb looked at her and said, "Me, too! I'm strong, too!"

Looking at both boys Mommy said, "Yes, you are strong. But you could be even stronger."

The boys next flew into the living room and Mommy followed them. Seeing a stuffed elephant on the floor, David remembered that superheroes could lift heavy objects. He called out proudly, "Look! I'm so strong I can lift an elephant!"

"Yes, you are strong, David. But you could be even stronger," Mommy said, as she tapped his nose lightly.

Caleb remembered that some superheroes could jump great distances from building to building. He stood on one couch and in a single leap jumped to the other couch. "I'm so strong I can jump super far!"

"Yes, you are strong, but you could be even stronger," Mommy said.

Caleb frowned, "But Mommy, we can fly and lift heavy things and jump far! We can't be stronger than that, can we?"

Mommy sat on the couch and Caleb climbed onto her lap. David sat next to them.

"There are many ways you can be strong, boys. But strength is more than big muscles, you see?"

Seeing the confused look on their faces, she smiled at them and continued to explain.

"Your strength *inside* makes you the strongest you can be."

Caleb looked up and said, "I want to be as strong as I can be!"

"Me, too," said David. "But what's the difference between inside strength and outside strength?"

"Outside strength is what others can easily see. When you use your muscles to pick things up or run around," said Mommy.

"What about inside strength?" asked Caleb.

"Well, let me ask you a question. Have you ever done something nice even when you didn't feel doing it?" asked Mommy.

David answered first. "Yesterday, I shared my truck with Sammy even though I really wanted to play with it all by myself."

"Exactly. And, Caleb, remember the time you kicked the soccer ball through Mrs. Johnson's basement window? Do you remember what you did?"

Caleb answered softly, "Daddy went with me and we knocked on her door, and then I said I was sorry. That was really hard. I was scared."

"I know you were scared, but you did the right thing anyway, honey. When you share a toy or say you're sorry—you show the world your *inside* strength."

"But doing that stuff is hard . . ." said Caleb.

"I know it is, Caleb. It's hard for David. It's hard for me. It's hard for everyone. That's why we all need inside strength."

Caleb crossed his arms and sighed. He always did that when he was trying to figure something out.

David asked her, "Since it's so hard, how can kids like me and Caleb get strong on the inside?"

"I'm glad you asked, David," Mommy smiled. "All we have to do is ask God to help us. God gives us the strength on the inside to do good."

"Even when it's really hard? Even if I don't want to?" Caleb asked.

"Yes," Mommy answered. "God is always with us. When we ask God for help, he gives us his special powers—his grace."

"Then, we can be superheroes! I can be Courageous Caleb! And he can be Daring David!" Caleb exclaimed, as the boys jumped down from the couch.

"We can all be superheroes when we ask God to give us his grace to make us strong inside and out. Because strength is more than big muscles, you see. Strength on the inside makes you the strongest you can be."

Just then, Courageous Caleb and Daring David ran to the window. They could see their soccer teammates gathering for their game.

"Mommy, is it time for our game?" asked Caleb.

"Sure is. Just grab your cleats and let's go," Mommy said.

During the game someone knocked Caleb down. David helped his cousin get up.

"Don't fight back, Caleb. Remember what your mom said: God gives us inside strength to do the right thing."

"You're right," said Caleb. "We'll just play a good game."

The game ended, when the other team scored the winning goal. Caleb and David were not happy that their team lost.

"I don't want to shake their hands," grumbled David.

"But being a good sport is the right thing to do. Let's use our inside strength to be good sports," said Caleb.

Mommy watched as Caleb and David shook the winning team members' hands. "Great game," they said to the other players.

As they walked across the field Caleb said, "Mommy, did you see? We used our outside and our inside strength!"

"Yes," Mommy said, grinning. "When you ran and kicked you showed your outside strength. And when you forgave someone for knocking you down and were good sports, you showed your inside strength."

The boys cheered and Caleb said, "God helped us do the right thing. We are strong inside and out. Now we're true superheroes!

"Strength is more than big muscles, you see. Strength on the inside makes us the strongest we can be."

For Grown-Ups

When my son was young, he would run around the house in his homemade cape, making zooming sounds and jumping from sofa to chair, pretending he had come to save the day. In his mind, he was a superhero. But one day when I saw him help a friend pick up spilled crayons at school, I realized that he was a true superhero—one who helps others and does the right thing.

In today's society, boys are seen as strong when they have big muscles, or are successful athletes. Many boys compare themselves to others and seek to demonstrate their strength in various—and not always appropriate—ways. At times, this can lead boys to seeing themselves as not being able to live up to these imaginary and often arbitrary standards and vewing themselves as weak.

As believers, we know that there are different kinds of strength. And both—internal and external—are gifts from God.

Mommy, Am I Strong? is intended to help parents and educators teach children that strength is not just physical. A person's inner strength can be seen in actions and choices. And, when we face difficult situations, we can ask God for the grace to give us the strength we need.

This book

★ explores strength from the perspective of little boys;
★ encourages children to recognize different types of strength;
★ empowers children to demonstrate inner strength through kind actions and virtuous choices.

Through engaging storytelling and colorful illustrations, this book helps children understand that they can be strong on the *inside* as well as the outside and that with God everyone can be a superhero!

Michelle S. Lazurek is a pastor's wife, mother, Bible teacher, author, and speaker who encourages ordinary people to become extraordinary disciples. Through the art of storytelling, Michelle writes books that inspire and teach children biblical values. In addition to *Mommy, Am I Strong?* Michelle has also written a book for girls titled *Daddy, Am I Beautiful?* (Pauline Books & Media 2015). Learn more about Michelle at www.michellelazurek.com.

Scott Spinks lives in west central Minnesota with his wife, Macushla, and their son, Hogan. Nestled comfortably in the front room of their home, he creates drawings, which are often inspired by the comic books and classic cartoons of his childhood. Scott also serves as a firefighter with the Long Lake Fire Department. To learn more about Scott, visit www.scottspinks.com.

Positively Human kids
Pauline

Our Positively Human Line offers an affirmative view of the human person while integrating faith concepts for kids.

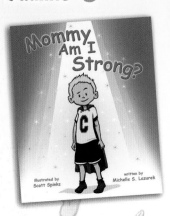

Mommy Am I Strong?
illustrated by Scott Spinks
written by Michelle S. Lazurek

Daddy, Am I Beautiful?
Written by Michelle S. Lazurek
Illustrated by Apryl Stott

God Has a Plan for Boys and for Girls
Written by Monica Ashour
Illustrated by Marilee Harrald-Pilz

Every Body Has Something to Say

Everybody Has Something to Give
Written by Monica Ashour
Illustrated by Marilee Harrald-Pilz

To find these and other delightful books for children, visit one of our **Pauline Books & Media Centers** listed on the last page or stop by: www.pauline.org. We'd love to hear from you!

Who are the Daughters of St. Paul?

We are Catholic sisters. Our mission is to be like Saint Paul and tell everyone about Jesus! There are so many ways for people to communicate with each other. We want to use all of them so everyone will know how much God loves us. We do this by printing books (you're holding one!), making radio shows, singing, helping people at our bookstores, using the internet, and in many other ways.

Visit our Web site at www.pauline.org

Pauline
BOOKS & MEDIA

The Daughters of St. Paul operate book and media centers
at the following addresses. Visit, call, or write the one nearest you today,
or find us at www.pauline.org.

CALIFORNIA
3908 Sepulveda Blvd, Culver City, CA 90230   310-397-8676
935 Brewster Avenue, Redwood City, CA 94063   650-369-4230
5945 Balboa Avenue, San Diego, CA 92111   858-565-9181

FLORIDA
145 SW 107th Avenue, Miami, FL 33174   305-559-6715

HAWAII
1143 Bishop Street, Honolulu, HI 96813   808-521-2731

ILLINOIS
172 North Michigan Avenue, Chicago, IL 60601   312-346-4228

LOUISIANA
4403 Veterans Memorial Blvd, Metairie, LA 70006   504-887-7631

MASSACHUSETTS
885 Providence Hwy, Dedham, MA 02026   781-326-5385

MISSOURI
9804 Watson Road, St. Louis, MO 63126   314-965-3512

NEW YORK
64 West 38th Street, New York, NY 10018   212-754-1110

SOUTH CAROLINA
243 King Street, Charleston, SC 29401   843-577-0175

TEXAS
Currently no book center; for parish exhibits or outreach evangelization,
contact: 210-569-0500 or SanAntonio@paulinemedia.com
or P.O. Box 761416, San Antonio, TX 78245

VIRGINIA
1025 King Street, Alexandria, VA 22314   703-549-3806

CANADA
3022 Dufferin Street, Toronto, ON M6B 3T5   416-781-9131

SMILE—*God loves you!*